Early years inspection handbook for Ofsted-registered provision

Updated 15 December 2021

This guidance applies from 1 September 2021.

GRAN*GIS* UK Publishing

Adapted and Published by GRANGIS (Grand Register Library).
Online: www.grangis.com.
E-mail: contact@grangis.com.

In this version:
ISBN: 979-8-88559-087-7

Note: Title, sub-title and version of this publication is as described.

Table of Contents

Early years inspection handbook for Ofsted-registered provision

Updated 15 December 2021

This guidance applies from 1 September 2021.

Introduction

1. This handbook describes the main activities that inspectors undertake when they carry out inspections of early years providers in England registered under sections 49 and 50 of the Childcare Act 2006. The handbook also sets out the judgements that inspectors will make and on which they will report.

2. The handbook has 2 parts:

- Part 1. How we will inspect Ofsted-registered early years providers: This contains instructions and guidance for inspectors on preparing for and carrying out early years registered inspections
- Part 2. The evaluation schedule: This contains guidance for inspectors on judging the quality and standards of Ofsted-registered early years settings and indicates the main types of evidence used

3. This handbook is available to providers and other organisations to make sure that they know about inspection processes and procedures. It balances the need for consistent inspection with the flexibility needed to respond to each provider's particular circumstances. It should be regarded as an explanation of normal procedures, as inspections will vary according to the evidence provided. This handbook applies to inspections carried out from September 2019 under the education inspection framework (EIF).

Privacy notice

4. During an inspection, inspectors will collect information about staff and children at the setting by looking at records and observing the everyday life of the setting. We use this information to prepare our report and for the purposes set out in our privacy policy.

5. We normally gather evidence electronically using a range of devices, including laptops, mobile telephones and tablets. All evidence is securely transferred to Ofsted's systems. These will be stored as evidence but not retained by the inspector personally.

Inspection and the COVID-19 (coronavirus) pandemic

6. This section outlines the additional considerations for inspectors when carrying out inspections of early years providers in the context of the COVID-19 pandemic and transitional period.[footnote 1] This section should be read alongside parts 1 and 2 of the inspection handbook. We will keep our handbook and methodology under review during the transitional period, as circumstances change and we continue to emerge from the pandemic.

7. This section sets out our approach to routine graded inspections. It covers how this will reflect the COVID-19 context and the disruption it has caused and may continue to cause to many education providers. It also covers the transitional period.

8. All inspections will be carried out on site. However, it may be pragmatic to do some elements of the inspection through video/telephone calls. This will be agreed with the provider at the start of the inspection. We will usually only use video/telephone calls to involve parents/carers and those with leadership responsibility who are unable to attend the setting.

Preparation and planning

9. During the notification phone call with the provider or its representative, the inspector will seek to understand the specific impact of COVID-19 on the provider and how leaders have responded to the situation.

10. In this conversation, the provider and inspector will agree safety protocols that the inspection team will follow to ensure that the inspection is completed in a COVID-19 secure way.

11. Given this additional discussion, the conversation may take longer than usual. It may be that all these elements are discussed in a single telephone conversation. Alternatively, they may be covered in 2 separate conversations with a break in between, as agreed between the inspector and the provider.

Reaching inspection judgements

12. Inspectors will always seek to understand the impact of the COVID-19 pandemic on providers and will take this into account when reaching final inspection judgements. In making their judgement about a provider's overall effectiveness, inspectors will take account of the 4 judgements: quality of education, personal development, behaviour and attitudes and leadership and management.

13. Inspectors understand that some providers will have been unable to support children in the usual way during the COVID-19 pandemic. Throughout the inspection, inspectors will seek to understand how the provider adapted and prioritised what it did to get the best results for children throughout this period. They will take this into account when making inspection judgements.

14. We recognise that the disruption to learning caused by the pandemic may have impacted on what children know, remember and can do. This could result in some children having a wider than usual range of starting points and gaps in their knowledge. Inspectors will pay close attention to how providers identify and address any of these delays and gaps.

15. When evaluating the quality of education, using the judgement criteria set out in paragraphs 188 to 190, inspectors will consider the extent to which leaders have designed an ambitious and well-sequenced curriculum. When considering the impact of the curriculum, inspectors will have due regard to any loss of learning the pandemic may have caused. However, inspectors will consider what the provider is doing to address any disruption to learning to ensure that children are well prepared for their next stage of education.

Leadership

16. Inspectors will seek to understand how leaders have adapted their approaches as a result of the COVID-19 pandemic, including the rationale for any new or modified ways of working.

Safeguarding and welfare

17. The COVID-19 pandemic increased safeguarding risks. Inspectors will consider how providers adapted approaches to safeguarding during the pandemic to make sure that:

- vulnerable children, including those with SEND, were encouraged to attend the provision
- safeguarding procedures remained effective both for those at home and those attending the provision

18. Inspectors will discuss how safeguarding arrangements have changed over time due to the pandemic, and how providers have made sure that they remain effective.

19. Inspectors recognise that the context in which providers operate has changed as a result of the pandemic. Therefore, inspectors will discuss attendance patterns with providers to understand how the pandemic specifically affected the individual setting. They will consider the specific context and steps that providers have taken to ensure the best possible standards for attendance.

EYFS requirements and previous modifications and/or disapplication

20. To support early years providers during the COVID-19 outbreak, in April 2020 the government temporarily disapplied and modified certain elements of the early years foundation stage (EYFS) statutory framework (see 'Early years foundation stage: coronavirus disapplications'). This included detail on where providers should have applied 'reasonable endeavours' and 'best endeavours', if they were relying on any modifications and disapplications.

21. Disapplications ended on 31 August 2021. Inspectors will consider any circumstances where providers were relying on modifications to and/or disapplications of the requirements (where applicable).

22. Inspectors will have due regard to any loss of learning the pandemic may have caused. Inspectors will consider what the provider is doing to address any disruption to learning to ensure that children are well prepared for their next stage of education.

23. When determining judgements, the inspector will consider all failures to meet EYFS requirements, even where they were previously modified (see guidance on disapplications and modifications). If the inspector judges the provision not to have an acceptable standard of care and/or quality of education, the overall effectiveness will be judged inadequate. When judging provision as inadequate, the inspector must decide whether the provider has the capacity to put things right through non-statutory actions or whether the failures are serious enough to warrant enforcement action (see paragraphs 126 to 140 for further information).

24. Assessment arrangements may also have been altered as a result of the pandemic. Inspectors will need to understand where providers may have previously relied on the modifications to some of the assessment requirements of the EYFS.[footnote 2]

25. Inspectors will check whether providers were meeting relevant assessment requirements They will also check how providers were supporting staff with any additional workload expectations as a result.

Revisions to the EYFS from 1 September 2021

26. In October 2019, the Department for Education (DfE) launched a public consultation seeking views on changes to the statutory framework for the EYFS. The consultation included proposed changes to the educational programmes, the early learning goals and the EYFS profile assessment.

27. All registered nurseries, childminders, schools and pre-schools in England must follow the revised and final EYFS framework from 1 September 2021.

28. 'Development matters', the DfE's non-statutory curriculum guidance to support the delivery of the revised EYFS statutory framework, is also being updated for use from 1 September. This guidance offers a top-level view of how children develop and learn, and guides, but does not replace, professional judgement.

29. We have also updated this handbook to reflect the revised EYFS. You can see a summary of the changes.

Part 1. How we will inspect early years providers registered with Ofsted

How we select providers for inspection

30. Once a provider is registered on the Ofsted Early Years Register, we carry out regular inspections to evaluate the overall quality and standards of its early years provision in line with the principles and requirements of the 'Statutory framework for the EYFS'.

31. The Parliamentary Under-Secretary of State for Children and Families wrote to Her Majesty's Chief Inspector (HMCI) on 3 November 2020 to outline inspection arrangements from the date that Ofsted resumes its full routine early years inspections. The letter states that Ofsted must inspect each provider within 6 years from the date of its last inspection. We will use the previous inspection judgement alongside any other information we hold about a provider to determine the timing of its next inspection. This aligns early years providers with other education remits.

32. Providers on the Early Years Register will normally be inspected at least once within a 6-year window. We will prioritise the first inspection of newly registered providers on the Early Years Register. This will normally be within 30 months of their registration date.

33. We prioritise inspections and/or inspect more frequently when we receive a concern about a setting, and risk assessment concludes that an inspection is needed.

34. All provision judged as inadequate will be re-inspected within 6 months.

35. All childminders, pre-school provision and nursery provision judged as requires improvement will usually be re-inspected within 12 months.

36. Provision that has been given 2 previous 'requires improvement' judgements is likely to be judged inadequate if there is no improvement at the next inspection. Provision that has been given 2 previous 'inadequate' judgements is likely to have its registration cancelled if there is no improvement at the next inspection. We usually also take steps to cancel a provider's registration at any point if we find that they are no longer meeting requirements.[footnote 3]

37. We risk-assess any information we receive about early years provision. This may remain on the provider's record or may be referred to the region for a decision on next steps. The region will decide whether to carry out an inspection, regulatory activity, or both. The nature of the concern will influence how quickly we inspect or visit. Depending on the urgency, regulatory activity may take place on the day the information is received. Information about regulatory activity is available in the early years compliance handbook.

38. Where the region decides to carry out an inspection as a result of the risk assessment, inspectors must, as part of the inspection, gather evidence that relates back to the concern. They should plan activities – including a discussion with the provider – and observations that enable them to gather sufficient evidence to complete the inspection. The provision may subsequently be judged to be outstanding, good, requires improvement or inadequate, according to the evidence, even if the inspection is taking place because of possible previous non-compliance. Judgements are not pre-determined. If a provider notifies us of an incident and uses the learning from it to improve the quality of the provision, this is generally considered to be a sign of a responsible provider. However, a number of notifications, particularly within a short space of time, or that relate to similar incidents, may be indicative of wider leadership weaknesses within the setting. The inspector should consider this when reaching their judgement.

39. When the inspection follows other regulatory action we have taken, the inspector should check that the provider is compliant with any actions or other enforcement measures that result from that previous action.

No children on roll or present on the day of inspection

40. Some childcare providers and childminders may have no children on roll at the time the inspection is carried out, or may not have any children present, even though they have children on roll.

41. In either circumstance, the inspection must not be deferred. However, if it becomes clear during the initial notification telephone call that the provider cares for children only on certain days or part-days, the inspection should be scheduled on a day where children are present, if practicable.[footnote 4] While the provider remains registered with us, they should expect to be inspected at any time.

42. Where there are no children on roll or present, the inspector must make it clear at the start of the inspection or during the initial notification telephone call that the inspection will not be a full inspection but will be a check that the provider continues to be suitable to remain registered. As a result, no grades will be given against the 4 key judgements. The inspector will make a judgement only on the 'Overall quality and standards of the early years provision', with one of 3 possible outcomes:

- met
- not met with actions
- not met with enforcement

43. Where a judgement is 'met', the inspector will not make recommendations. However, an inspector may reference within the report what the setting needs to do better.

44. If the provider does not meet one or more of the learning and development requirements and/or safeguarding and welfare requirements, the inspector must consider a judgement of 'not met' and either issue actions for the provider to take or consider enforcement action. In these cases, the inspector must follow the guidance for inadequate judgements set out later in this handbook.

45. The majority of inspections affected by no children on roll will be of childminders. A small number may be childcare providers. The main purpose of the inspection is to fulfil our legal duty to inspect registered providers within a defined period and to report in writing on certain matters. The inspection will report on whether the provider continues to demonstrate suitability to remain on the Early Years Register and, if applicable, the Childcare Register.

46. For these inspections, the inspector must assess whether the provider:

- has premises suitable for the education and care of children
- can demonstrate sufficient understanding of the EYFS requirements
- is able to meet the care, learning and development needs of children

47. Providers must confirm that they meet the requirements of the Childcare Register, if applicable.

48. The provider must demonstrate how they will:

- meet the learning and development requirements, if appropriate[footnote 5]
- meet the safeguarding and welfare requirements
- develop and deliver the educational programmes, if appropriate
- identify children's starting points and ensure that children make progress in their learning through effective planning, observation and assessment, if appropriate
- safeguard children
- work in partnership with parents, carers and others
- offer an inclusive service
- evaluate their service and strive for continuous improvement

49. The provider should tell the inspector how they have addressed any actions and/or recommendations from the last inspection and how this will improve the provision for children's care and learning.

50. If, during the inspection, the provider decides to resign from the Early Years Register and remain registered only on the Childcare Register, the inspector must collect sufficient evidence of compliance with the Childcare Register requirements by referring to the 'Childcare Register requirements: childcare providers on non-domestic or domestic premises'.

Early years or childcare provision on a school site

51. Schools that take children aged 2 years and over as part of their early years provision cannot normally register that provision with Ofsted.[footnote 6] We will inspect the provision for these children under the school inspection arrangements.

52. Schools that take children younger than 2 years must register with Ofsted. We will inspect this provision under the early years inspection arrangements set out in this handbook.

Before the inspection

Clarification for providers

53. The information below confirms our requirements. This is to dispel myths about inspection that can result in unnecessary workload for providers. It is intended to highlight specific practices that we do not require. More detail on what evidence inspectors will gather can be found in paragraph 84.

54. Ofsted will:

- when making judgements, take a range of evidence into account, including: discussions with leaders, staff and children; the joint learning walk; observations; speaking to parents and so on (see paragraphs 82 to 84
- judge fairly providers that take different approaches to meeting the requirements of the EYFS; inspectors will assess any provider's curriculum favourably when leaders have built or adopted a curriculum with appropriate coverage, content, structure and sequencing and implemented it effectively.

55. Ofsted will not:

- create unnecessary workload for staff through its recommendations
- advocate a particular method of planning, teaching or assessment; it is up to providers to determine their practices and it is up to leaders to

justify these on their own merits rather than by referring to this handbook.

56. Ofsted does not require providers to:

- provide EYFS curriculum planning in any specific format for inspection
- prepare any performance and children-tracking information for Ofsted
- do additional work or to ask children to do work specifically for the inspection.

Inspectors' planning and preparation

57. The inspector must prepare for the inspection by gaining a broad overview of the setting, its context and history. As part of this preparation, inspectors must check and evaluate information to inform their areas of inspection focus.

58. As part of their preparation, inspectors must consider:

- which register(s) the provider is on and confirm that we hold the correct registered/legal entity details; if there is any uncertainty about the registration, the inspector must contact their regional duty desk and try to resolve the issue promptly; if this is not possible, the inspector may delay carrying out the inspection until the matter is resolved
- the accuracy of the information about individuals connected with the registration
- all the information held on our database
- details of any concerns received and specifically those they have been asked to follow up
- previous inspection reports
- any published information, such as outcome summaries and monitoring letters
- the progress the provider has made with any actions or recommendations raised at the last inspection or visit
- the provider's website, if they have one
- the internet, to see whether there are any safeguarding or other issues relating to the provider that may need to be followed up during the inspection
- any other contextual information we may hold about the provider or the setting

59. Inspectors must update the information about the setting in their evidence base and agree this with the provider at the start of the inspection.

60. Inspectors must take account of the provider's regulatory history when planning the inspection and note any concerns in their evidence. These will normally be shared with the provider.

Notification of inspection

61. Group provision will normally receive a telephone call at around midday on the working day before the start of the inspection.

62. In group provision, if the provider or their representative is unavailable when the inspection notification call is made to the setting, the inspector should ask to speak to the most senior member of staff available.

63. If all reasonable steps have been taken to make contact with the setting but the inspector has not been able to speak to anyone, then the inspection will continue the following day without notice.

64. Childminders, or group providers that do not operate regularly, such as summer play schemes, will usually receive a call no more than 5 days before the inspection to check which days they are operating and whether there are children on roll and present.[footnote 7] The inspector must not specify any proposed dates for the inspection but should indicate the time of day the inspection will start. This will allow the childminder to leave the house if the inspector has not arrived by that time.

65. The telephone call is the first opportunity to initiate a professional relationship between the inspector and the provider or their representative. It should be short and focused on practical issues. Inspectors should not use this conversation to start inspecting. The purpose of the notification call is to provide an opportunity for the setting to ask questions about the inspection and to confirm that:

- the setting is aware of Ofsted's privacy notice
- the setting's registration status and clarify any issues relating to the registration
- the setting knows about its statutory duty to inform parents of the inspection
- arrangements for the inspection; this includes informing the provider or their representative (normally the manager) that they will usually be required to take part in joint observations
- discussions with particular staff members, including the manager or the named deputy in the manager's absence
- the nominated person, where appropriate, giving them the opportunity to be present at the feedback meeting
- that relevant documents are made available as soon as possible from the start of the inspection (see paragraph 66)
- the age range of children, numbers on roll and the times at which the setting is open and any other contextual information
- whether the setting provides any funded places and/or receives early years pupil premium funding (see paragraph 83)
- any additional support and/or arrangements for children who need special educational provision, including responses to any emerging needs or difficulties,[footnote 8] or whether any children attending the setting

are subject to a child protection plan or child in need plan (see paragraph 83)

66. Inspectors should tell the provider that the relevant documentation or information they must access includes:

- paediatric first-aid certificates
- the Disclosure and Barring Service (DBS) records and any other documents summarising the checks on, and the vetting and employment arrangements of, all staff working at the setting

67. Inspectors should tell the provider that the relevant documentation or information they may need access to includes: (see paragraphs 53 to 56)

- a list of current staff and their qualifications
- a register/list showing the date of birth of all children on roll and routine staffing arrangements
- a list of children present at the setting during the inspection (if not shown on the register)
- all logs that record accidents, exclusions, children taken off roll and incidents of poor behaviour
- all logs of incidents of discrimination, including racist incidents
- complaints log and/or evidence of any complaints and their resolutions
- safeguarding and child protection policies
- fire-safety arrangements and other statutory policies relating to health and safety
- a list of any referrals made to the local authority designated person for safeguarding, with brief details of the resolutions
- details of all children who are an open case to social care/children's services and for whom there is a multi-agency plan

68. Childminders are not required to provide inspectors with written policies and procedures but must be able to explain them in relation to the requirements in the EYFS.

Requests for deferral or rescheduled inspection

69. If a setting requests a deferral of its inspection, the inspector must immediately tell the regional duty desk. We will decide whether the request should be granted in line with our deferral policy. The absence of the provider or manager, or having no children on roll, are not valid reasons for deferral. Decisions will be made on a case-by-case basis.

70. Where possible, a setting that has no children present on the planned day of inspection, but is operating at other times during the week, should have its inspection rescheduled for one of those days.

71. Inspections that are prioritised as a result of risk assessment will not usually be deferred, even if there are no children on roll or present at the time of the visit.

Inspection without prior notification

72. We may carry out inspections without notice. This normally, but not exclusively, happens when a provider has been judged as inadequate at its last inspection or when the region decides to carry out an inspection, as a result of a risk assessment. We prioritise inspections of settings that are judged as inadequate and/or because of concerns that have been expressed about a setting. When the inspection is carried out without notice, the inspector will:

- introduce themselves and show the provider their identification; the inspector must allow the provider time to look at their identification and to contact us to confirm the identity of the inspector should they wish to do so
- ask the provider to display the notice of inspection so that parents are aware that an inspection is taking place
- make arrangements to talk to parents; this may be almost immediately if parents are present
- confirm the accuracy of – or any changes to – the information about the setting
- agree a timetable for inspection activities, including joint observations
- carry out a learning walk of the premises and follow up any issues that arise
- check the DBS records and any other documents summarising the checks on, and the vetting and employment arrangements of, all staff working at the setting
- check staff qualifications, including paediatric first aid, and record them in their evidence base
- arrange meetings with the provider and/or their representative at a mutually convenient time during the inspection
- refer to any concerns that have led to the inspection being prioritised, remaining mindful of the need to maintain confidentiality and to protect sensitive information and the identities of any complainants
- arrange meetings with staff

Safeguarding

73. Inspectors will always have regard to how well children are helped and protected so that they are kept safe. Although inspectors will not provide a separate grade for this crucial aspect of a provider's work, they will always make

a written judgement in the report about whether the arrangements for safeguarding children are effective.

74. We have published a document that sets out the approach inspectors should take to inspecting safeguarding in all the settings covered by the framework. It should be read alongside the EYFS and the early years handbook:

- 'Inspecting safeguarding in early years, education and skills settings'

75. It is also essential that inspectors are familiar with and take into account the statutory guidance in relation to safeguarding:

- 'Working together to safeguard children'

Where the expectations in the 'Inspecting safeguarding in the early years, education and skills settings' differ from those set out in the EYFS, settings should follow the EYFS requirements.

During the inspection

Days allocated to inspection and inspection team members

76. The time spent on inspection normally depends on the size of the provision. Most inspections are carried out by one inspector.

77. When inspecting:

- a childminder, the inspector will normally be on site for about 3 hours
- group provision that operates only for restricted daily hours, the inspector will normally be present for about 4 hours
- group provision open for a full day, the inspector will normally be on site for at least 6 hours
- the inspection may be carried out by more than one inspector or be carried out over more than one day, at the discretion of the region

The start of the on-site inspection

78. On entering the setting, inspectors must introduce themselves and show the provider their identification. The inspector must allow the provider time to check the identification and to contact us to confirm it, should they wish to do so. In group settings, the inspector must ensure that the provider has been informed of their arrival.

79. The inspector should meet the provider or representative briefly on arrival to confirm arrangements for the inspection, including:

- checking the accuracy of – or any changes to – the information about the setting
- gathering any information about staff absences, children on roll and other practical matters[footnote 9]
- asking the provider to display the notice of inspection – if this has not already been done – so that parents are aware that an inspection is taking place
- agreeing the timetable for inspection activities, including a learning walk; joint observations; inspectors must offer the provider or their representative the opportunity to take part in joint observations and their response must be recorded
- making arrangements for a longer meeting at a convenient time with the provider or their representative to discuss the setting's evaluation of the quality of provision and other matters relating to leadership and management
- making arrangements for providing feedback at the end of the inspection and, for group provision, request that the nominated individual or their representative is invited
- making arrangements to talk to parents – this may be almost immediately if parents are present – and to check that the provider has informed them about the inspection
- checking staff qualifications and record them in the evidence base

80. If the inspection is being carried out without notice, the inspector should refer to any concerns that have led to the inspection taking place. The inspector should be aware of the need to maintain confidentiality and to protect fully any sensitive information relating to complainants.

81. If there is more than one inspector, a short team meeting should clarify inspection activities, the areas to be explored initially and individual roles and responsibilities.

Gathering and recording evidence

82. During inspections, inspectors will carry out the following activities:

- joint observation

- observing children
- learning walk
- discussions with leaders/managers

These activities enable inspectors to gather evidence to make valid and reliable inspection judgements. These activities, part of our inspection methodology, are an effective way of finding out what it is like for a child at that setting or with that childminder. Paragraphs 53 to 56 dispel myths about inspection that can result in unnecessary workload in providers.

83. Inspectors will evaluate evidence of the impact of the curriculum, including on the most disadvantaged children. Disadvantaged children includes children with SEND (see paragraph 65). It also includes children who meet the criteria for the provider to receive early years pupil premium funding.

84. Inspectors must spend as much time as possible gathering evidence about the quality of care, teaching and learning by:

- observing the children at play
- talking to the children and practitioners about the activities provided
- talking to parents to gain their views on the quality of care and education provided
- observing the interactions between practitioners and children
- gauging children's levels of understanding and their engagement in learning
- talking to practitioners about their assessment of what children know and can do and how they are building on it
- observing care routines and how they are used to support children's personal development, including the setting's approach to toilet training
- evaluating the practitioners' knowledge of the EYFS curriculum

85. In group provision, the inspector must track a representative sample of 2 or more children across the inspection. The inspector should discuss with the provider what they intend the relevant children to learn and remember based on what those children know and can already do. The evidence collected must refer to:

- the practitioner's knowledge of each child
- the progress check for any children aged 2
- the impact of any early years pupil premium funding on the children's development
- the quality of support for any children with SEND (see paragraph 65)
- the discussions held with each child's key person and how they decide what to teach
- how well children are developing in the prime and specific areas of learning that help them to be ready for their next stage of education, including school
- the reason why children may not receive their full entitlement to early education and the impact that has on them, particularly those from disadvantaged backgrounds and those with SEND (see paragraph 65)

If any of the children are eligible for the early years pupil premium (see paragraph 83) or subject to a child protection plan or child in need plan, at least one of them must be included in the sample of those tracked.

86. As childminders have only a small number of children, inspectors are not able to track a sample of children in the same way. Nevertheless, the same principles apply in terms of evaluating the childminder's practice and its impact on children's learning, development and well-being.

87. Inspectors must record their evidence clearly and succinctly. All sections of the evidence base must be completed before the end of the inspection. Inspectors may make handwritten notes, but these must be transferred to the electronic evidence as soon as possible after the end of the inspection. It is essential that the evidence accurately reflects discussions with staff and managers. Individuals can be named in inspection evidence if it is necessary to identify them and to avoid confusion. Inspectors should identify clearly any information that was provided in confidence.

88. The evidence underpinning the judgements and areas for improvement must be used to summarise the main points for feedback and to write the report.

89. The electronic evidence and any handwritten notes may be scrutinised for the purposes of retrieval or quality assurance monitoring or as a source of evidence in the event of a complaint or a Freedom of Information request.

Using the setting's own analysis of its strengths and weaknesses during the inspection

90. Leaders and managers of settings should have an accurate view of the quality of their provision and know what to improve. They do not need to produce a written self-evaluation but should be prepared to discuss the quality of education and care they provide – and how well they meet the needs of the children – with the inspector. Inspectors will consider how well leaders and managers evaluate their provision and know how they can improve it or maintain its high standards.

91. The inspector must meet the provider or their representative to discuss how they evaluate their practice. Normally, the discussion should be at a point in the inspection that gives the inspector enough time to follow up any matters discussed. To test the accuracy of the setting's analysis, the inspector will observe children learning, staff caring and teaching, and the safety and suitability of the premises. The inspector will discuss how the provider evaluates the quality of its provision, checking whether they take account of the views of parents and the progress made by the children to determine what it needs to improve.

92. During the inspection, inspectors will use the information provided to test whether the provider's view of the quality of the setting is realistic and to gauge what needs to improve.

Observation and discussion

93. Inspectors will complete a learning walk around the premises with the provider or their representative early on in the inspection. This provides an opportunity for leaders to explain how they organise the early years provision, including the aims and rationale for their EYFS curriculum.

94. Inspectors must discuss with leaders and practitioners what they intend children to learn, know and do as a result of the EYFS curriculum they offer. They must follow this discussion through in their observations and discussions with children at play and staff interactions.

95. Inspectors must not advocate a particular method of planning, teaching or assessment. They must not look for a preferred methodology but must record aspects of teaching and learning that they observe to be effective and identify what needs to improve.

96. Inspectors will not analyse a provider's internal progress and attainment data during an inspection. This does not mean that providers cannot use data where they consider it appropriate. Inspectors will, however, put more focus on the curriculum and less on a provider's generation, analysis and interpretation of data. Leaders and managers have told us they believe this will help us play our part in reducing unnecessary workload. Inspectors will be interested in the conclusions drawn and actions taken from any internal assessment information, but they will not examine or verify that information first-hand. Inspectors will, however, ask providers to explain why they have decided to collect whatever assessment data they collect, what they are drawing from their data and how that informs their curriculum and teaching.

97. Inspectors do not expect to see documentation other than that set out in the EYFS. They will use the evidence gathered from discussions and their own observations to help judge the overall quality of the curriculum provided for children.

98. Inspectors must spend most of the inspection time gathering first-hand evidence by observing the quality of the daily routines and activities of children and staff. These observations enable inspectors to judge the contribution practitioners make to children's learning, progress, safety and well-being. The observations should also enable them to collect sufficient evidence to support detailed and specific recommendations about improvements needed to the quality of education, behaviour and attitudes, personal development, and leadership and management.

99. In group settings, inspectors should observe as many staff as possible to ensure that an accurate picture of the overall quality of interactions between practitioners and children can be gained.

100. When observing interactions between staff and children, inspectors should consider how well staff:

- engage in dialogue with children
- watch, listen and respond to children
- model language well
- read aloud and tell stories to children
- encourage children to sing songs, nursery rhymes and musical games
- encourage children to express their thoughts and use new words
- support independence and confidence
- encourage children to speculate and test ideas through trial and error
- enable children to explore and solve problems
- behave as an excellent role model for children
- support children to recognise and respond to their own physical needs
- attend to children's personal needs
- deal with children's care arrangements, including intimate care, the levels of privacy afforded to children and the supervision arrangements when undertaking personal hygiene tasks

101. Inspectors will also discuss children's learning and development with staff as part of the inspection. There will be a particular focus on communication and language, as the development of children's spoken language underpins all 7 areas of learning and development that are set out in paragraph 1.6 of the statutory framework for the EYFS. Much of this will be through incidental conversations prompted by observing the children at play and the interactions between them and adults.

102. Where the quality of practice is weak, the inspector must talk to the provider about what has been observed. The inspector should also ask about any action the provider is taking to bring about improvement.

103. The inspector should always invite the provider or a nominated senior member of staff – such as the manager or early years professional – to take part in one or more joint observations of activities, care routines and/or scrutiny of the progress children make. If the provider declines the opportunity to take part in joint observations, this should be recorded in the evidence base, along with the reason given.

104. Joint observations should enable the inspector to:

- gain an insight into the effectiveness of the provision's professional development programme for practitioners
- learn about the provider's view of staff's interactions with children
- see the quality of the implementation of the curriculum/educational programmes

- consider how effectively the manager supports staff to promote the learning and development of all children

105. Following a joint observation, the inspector should discuss and note any similarities or differences between the provider's evaluation and their own.

106. When childminders work alone, it is not possible to carry out joint observations in the same way. However, it is possible for the inspector and childminder to observe individual children together and discuss their learning, progress and behaviour as part of the activities that the children are engaged in. The inspector should follow this up with a further discussion about what the child has learned and how the childminder intends to build on it to help the child make progress. If childminders have assistants, a joint observation of one assistant may be possible.

Evaluating policies and procedures

107. Childcare providers are required to have policies and procedures, as set out in the EYFS. Childminders are not required to have written policies, but they must make sure that they have effective procedures in place as set out in the EYFS. They must ensure that any assistants are aware of and follow the statutory policies and can explain them to parents and others when requested.

108. All providers, including childminders, are expected to keep any written records in English.

109. The EYFS is clear that records must be easily accessible and available (these may be kept securely off the premises). Records required by the safeguarding and welfare requirements of the EYFS must be easily accessible and available by the end of any visit or inspection, as appropriate.

110. In addition to meeting the EYFS requirements, providers must comply with other legislation. This includes legislation relating to safeguarding, employment, anti-discrimination, health and safety, and data processing and storage. If the inspector identifies concerns that may relate to other legislation, they must notify the regional duty desk. A decision will then be made about what action should be taken and whether there should be liaison with the other agencies.

111. The inspector must check all DBS records and paediatric first-aid certificates, and record in the evidence base that they have done so.

112. Inspectors are unlikely to check all policies held by the provider. However, they should consider:

- recruitment records

- staff qualifications and deployment
- staff training for safeguarding practice and procedures
- records of complaints

113. The inspector is likely to talk to leaders and staff about how they implement their policies in practice, particularly where it relates to the training and development of staff. Where potential non-compliance with the EYFS is identified, inspectors are likely to check staff's knowledge of the setting's policies.

Meetings with parents

114. Wherever possible, the inspector must find out the views of parents during the inspection, including those of any parents who ask to speak to them. This will contribute to judgements about how well the provision works in partnership with parents to support children's learning and development, and the promotion of their well-being.

115. Where the provision has been notified in advance, parents will know that an inspection is taking place. The inspector should consider the arrival times of children and parents to the setting and should set aside time to speak to parents.

116. If the inspection is carried out with no notice, the inspector must check how the provider obtains and uses their views to improve its service. If there is no evidence relating to this, the inspector must consider whether the partnership with parents is good enough and the inspector may choose to contact parents by phone to request their views.

Meeting with the provider and/or their representative

117. The inspector must meet the provider or, if the provider is not present, the manager. The inspector should consider the best time to hold this meeting. It should be early enough in the inspection so that matters that are being discussed can be followed up.

118. If the provision operates from one room or in the provider's home, the meeting will need to take place at appropriate moments during the general observations, when the children are safely occupied. The inspector should be mindful that the provider has to supervise children and continue to meet their needs during any meeting time.

119. If the provider is not working directly with children and the meeting takes place in a room or office where the inspector cannot see the provision, it should take no longer than one hour. In most cases, it will be much shorter. The main evidence must come from direct observation of children.

120. The inspector should hold brief discussions with the provider to discuss the findings that are emerging during the inspection and record all these in the inspection evidence.

121. Before the inspection is complete, the inspector should always check with the provider whether further evidence should be taken into account. If the evidence suggests that the provision might be inadequate, the inspector should give the provider an opportunity to offer further evidence by having early discussions about this.

122. The inspector should seek to identify where improvements are needed and make recommendations about how the provision might improve.

Performance management and professional development

123. Inspectors will gather evidence of the effectiveness of staff supervision, performance management, training and continuing professional development, and the impact of these on children's well-being, learning and development. This includes evidence on how effectively leaders engage with staff and make sure they are aware of and manage any of the main pressures on them.

124. The early years sector is diverse, ranging from single childminders to large day-care settings. This means that inspectors must use their professional judgement to assess how well the provider improves the quality of provision.

125. Inspectors should consider how effectively senior leaders use performance management and their assessment of strengths and areas for improvement within the setting to provide a focus for professional development activities, particularly in relation to increasing children's vocabulary and cultural capital.

Reaching final judgements

126. Paragraphs 12 to 15 set out our approach to reaching final judgements within the COVID-19 context.

127. Inspection activity, including observations, should continue throughout the inspection. Inspectors should avoid giving any impression that they have reached final judgements before the inspection has finished.

128. The inspector must set aside sufficient time towards the end of the inspection to consider the evidence and make the final judgements. Final judgement grades should be recorded and the main points for feedback should be identified. The inspector should also ensure that time is set aside for the final feedback meeting.

129. Part 2 of this handbook sets out the judgements that the inspector must make and the aspects they should consider when doing so. The inspector must use professional judgement to weigh up the evidence gathered for each key judgement. It should be considered against the descriptors to reach fair and reliable judgements that reflect the quality of the provision.

130. Actions and recommendations for improvement should make clear what the provider needs to do to improve. Actions must refer to the requirements in the EYFS but should not simply repeat its wording. Recommendations for settings judged good or requiring improvement must focus on what the setting needs to do better. The inspector is not expected to check that each of the statutory requirements set out in the EYFS are met. However, if, in the course of collecting evidence, the inspector finds that a particular requirement is not met, they should take this into account when reaching judgements.

131. If one or more of the statutory requirements is not being met, this should be reflected in the judgement on leadership and management, as well as in any other judgements where it is relevant.

132. Failure to meet a statutory requirement will not always result in a judgement that the provision is inadequate. Where a statutory requirement is not met, the inspector will take into account the impact of this on children's health, safety and well-being as well as their learning and development.

133. Where the quality of education judgement is judged to be less than good, the overall effectiveness judgement will normally not be higher. There does not need to be a failure to meet a statutory requirement of the EYFS for a setting to be judged as less than good.

134. When a provision does not meet statutory requirements at the time of the inspection, the inspector must take into account any previous non-compliance. A provider may commit a series of minor breaches to EYFS requirements that, taken individually, do not have a significant impact on children's health, safety or welfare or their learning and development. However, a history of previous non-compliance in the same, or different, areas is likely to indicate either that the provider lacks knowledge of the requirements or is unwilling to comply with them. In such cases, the inspector is likely to judge the leadership and management to be inadequate because the provider does not understand the statutory requirements sufficiently.

135. Minor administrative errors that can be put right before the inspection is over should not necessarily have a negative impact on the judgements. An example might be that the certificate of registration is not properly displayed (paragraph 3.76 of the 'Statutory framework for the EYFS). However, where the provider is not meeting a number of administrative requirements, the inspector will need to consider whether these failings, taken together, suggest wider weaknesses within the setting. If this is the case, it is likely to have a negative impact on the leadership and management judgement.

136. The inspector must take account of all failures to meet EYFS requirements when determining the judgements. If the inspector judges the provision not to have an acceptable standard of care and/or quality of education, the overall effectiveness will be judged inadequate. When judging provision as inadequate, the inspector must decide whether the provider has the capacity to put things right through non-statutory actions or whether the failures are serious enough to warrant enforcement action.

137. Where a provider is not meeting statutory requirements but the inspector judges that leadership has the capacity to remedy this quickly, actions will be set. The actions will be listed in the inspection report. The inspector should raise actions if they find that:

- the provider is not meeting one or more of the learning and development requirements and/or safeguarding and welfare requirements
- leaders and managers demonstrate an understanding of the requirements and show that they have the ability to make the necessary improvements without the need for statutory enforcement action

138. When there is a significant failure to meet the safeguarding and welfare requirements, inspectors will normally issue a welfare requirements notice. Inspectors will not normally issue an additional actions letter because any actions will usually be written in the inspection report. Inspectors are likely to issue a welfare requirements notice when a provider is failing to meet one or more of the safeguarding and welfare requirements that has a significant impact on children's health, safety and well-being. This is normally where one or more of the following apply:

- leaders and managers do not demonstrate their understanding of how to meet the safeguarding and welfare requirements of the EYFS
- there have been previous occasions of non-compliance in relation to the same or different requirement(s)
- actions relating to existing failures to meet safeguarding and welfare requirements have not been completed satisfactorily
- the failure to meet the requirement is so serious that the inspector judges that a welfare requirements notice is appropriate

139. On making the judgement that the provision is inadequate, the inspector must consult with the regional duty desk if:

- there is evidence of any immediate risk to children or failure to meet any of the conditions placed on the registration
- previous concerns about the provision have not been dealt with in a satisfactory way, including the failure to take satisfactory action to meet actions and/or welfare requirements set at a previous visit
- the inspector considers that they may need to issue a welfare requirements notice or take other enforcement action, such as suspension, cancellation or prosecution
- the provider shows insufficient understanding of their responsibility to meet the safeguarding and welfare and/or learning and development requirements of the EYFS
- the last inspection resulted in a judgement that the overall effectiveness was inadequate

140. The purpose of the inspector's consultation with the regional duty desk is to discuss whether – and what type of – enforcement action should be taken and the kind of monitoring that will be required. The early years compliance handbook has more information about enforcement options and the arrangements for following up enforcement activity. The discussion will determine what the inspection report will say about the enforcement action.

Failure to notify Ofsted and/or meet conditions

141. It is an offence to fail to notify Ofsted of a significant event or fail to comply with a condition of registration, without good reason. Where the inspector finds non-compliance, they must refer to the compliance handbook and contact the regional duty desk if necessary. The inspector should not set actions for breaches of condition or a failure to notify Ofsted about a significant event. However, the inspector must note any such failure in the report. Where appropriate, this may contribute to an inadequate judgement overall.

Providing feedback

142. Towards the end of the inspection the inspector should talk to the provider to:

- discuss any inadequate or outstanding practice they have seen
- ensure that the provider understands how the evidence supports the judgements
- allow the provider to raise any concerns, including those related to the conduct of the inspection or the inspector

- alert the provider to any serious concerns that may lead to the provision being judged inadequate

143. At the end of the inspection, there must be a feedback meeting that should include the provider and/or their representative. If the provider is not able to attend, the inspector should give feedback to the manager as the provider's representative. The inspector must not defer feedback to another day.

144. The inspector should allow enough preparation time for feedback, making sure that their evidence is clear and fully supports the judgements. They should be ready to provide examples that illustrate the provision's strengths and weaknesses.

145. At the feedback meeting, the inspector should explain that its purpose is to share the main findings of the inspection and any areas for improvement. The inspector must make it clear that the findings are restricted and confidential to the relevant senior personnel and that they must remain so until the provider receives the final report. If the provision is judged to be inadequate, however, the provider must inform the local authority immediately after the inspection.

146. Feedback notes must be consistent with the evidence discussed with the provider and the content of the report, and should cover the strengths and areas for improvement about:

- quality of education
- behaviour and attitudes
- personal development
- leadership and management
- actions and/or recommendations for improvement

147. The inspector must ensure that the provider or their representative is clear about the grades awarded for each judgement. The inspector should:

- refer to specific evidence if any judgements differ from the provider's view of the provision's strengths and areas for improvement
- state clearly the areas that are judged as inadequate and the reasons for this
- explain the areas for improvement and be prepared to discuss these with the provider so that they understand what should or must be improved and the reasons why
- state that the grades are provisional and so may be subject to change as a result of quality assurance procedures and should, therefore, be treated as restricted and confidential until the provider receives a copy of the inspection report (except in the case of an inadequate judgement where the provider should inform the local authority)
- where relevant, set out the next steps for provision judged as requires improvement or inadequate
- provide information about making a complaint about the inspection

148. The inspector should summarise in the evidence base the main points raised at the feedback meeting and the responses to these.

Before- and after-school care and holiday provision

149. Providers (including childminders) who only offer care before and after school or during the school holidays for children who normally attend Reception (or older) classes during the school day do not have to meet the learning and development requirements for those children. For children younger than Reception age, the provider must have regard to, but does not have to meet, the learning and development requirements. In both cases, this means they only have to meet the safeguarding and welfare requirements of the EYFS. The arrangements for inspecting this type of provision are set out in Annex A.

Provision that primarily educates children in their home language

150. Provision that educates children primarily through the medium of their home language must show inspectors that individuals have a sufficient grasp of English to ensure the children's well-being. For example, providers must demonstrate that, where necessary, they could summon help in English in an emergency or keep records required by the EYFS in English and share them with inspectors. They must also be able to read and understand safety instructions, other instructions, information about the administration of medication and information about food allergies.

151. If children are not developing a good standard of spoken English, inspectors will consider the impact on their progress and whether this might lead to a judgement that the overall quality of the provision is inadequate.

Exemptions from the learning and development requirements of the EYFS

152. Some providers will be exempt from some or all aspects of the learning and development requirements of the EYFS.[footnote 10] The exemptions may modify or fully exempt providers from delivering the educational programmes, meeting

individual learning goals and making the assessment arrangements. During the inspection, inspectors should find out if this is the case after reviewing the associated paperwork, which must include confirmation from the DfE that the provider is exempt and the extent of any such exemption. Inspectors should use their professional judgement in applying the grade descriptors in these cases and report accordingly. They should expect to gather evidence for the parts of the learning and development requirements that are not exempt.

After the inspection

Arrangements for publishing the report

153. The inspector present is responsible for writing the inspection report and submitting the evidence to Ofsted shortly after the inspection ends. The text of the report should explain the judgements and reflect the evidence. The findings in the report should be consistent with the feedback given to the provider at the end of the inspection. The report will explain what it is like to attend the early years setting.

154. When writing a report relating to an inspection that was prioritised, inspectors should ensure that it explains why the inspection took place and should report accordingly.

155. Where no children are on roll or present at the time of the inspection, inspectors must include a judgement of met/not met only for overall effectiveness. Although there will be no separate supporting judgements, the summary of main findings for parents on the front page must include at least one bullet point for each judgement in the evaluation schedule. The summary must also describe clearly any weaknesses that led to a 'not met' judgement.

Other information to be completed following an inspection

156. As well as submitting the report and evidence, the inspector must update our database with the following information:

- the number of places the registered provider offers and the ages of children attending
- the level and number of qualifications, including paediatric first aid, held by staff at the setting
- any previous actions that are complete and need to be closed
- any new actions or recommendations
- any changes to the people connected with the registration, including a note of any failure to notify us of changes
- any errors in the registration details, including those relating to the registered person and the register(s) on which the provider is placed

157. Inspection reports will be quality assured before we send a draft to the provider. In most circumstances, the provider will receive the draft report within 18 working days after the end of the inspection. The draft report is restricted and confidential to the relevant personnel (as determined by the provider), and should not be shared more widely or published. We may share a draft of the inspection report with the DfE and other bodies as necessary. This will only take place following moderation or quality assurance.

158. The provider will have 5 working days to comment on the draft report, inspection process and findings. We will consider all comments, and we will respond to the comments when we share the final report with the provider within 30 working days after the inspection.

159. The provider will have 5 working days to submit a formal complaint after we have shared the final report with them. If a complaint is not submitted, the report will normally be published on Ofsted's website 3 working days later. If a complaint has been submitted, the publication of the report may be delayed.

160. Paragraph 3.75 of the Statutory framework for the EYFS requires all early years providers to supply a copy of the inspection report to the parents of children attending on a regular basis.

The inspection evidence base

161. The evidence base must be retained in line with Ofsted's retention and disposal policy. This is normally 6 years from when the report is published. We may decide that retaining it for longer is warranted for research purposes and inspection evidence must be kept for longer than 6 years when:

- an action relates to safeguarding
- the provision is being monitored or regulatory action is linked to the inspection
- there is a potential or current litigation claim against Ofsted, such as a judicial review

- the inspection is of a very sensitive nature or is likely to be of national or regional importance due to a high level of political or press interest
- there is an appeal against enforcement action or an ongoing complaint
- it has been identified for research and evaluation purposes

Quality assurance and complaints

Quality assurance

162. All inspectors are responsible for the quality of their work. The inspector present must ensure that inspections are carried out in accordance with the principles of inspections and our code of conduct.

163. We monitor the quality of inspections through a range of formal processes and inspectors visit some providers or monitor remotely to quality assure inspections. We may also evaluate the quality of an inspection evidence base. If there is more than one inspector, the lead inspector will be responsible for giving team inspectors feedback about the quality of their work and their conduct.

164. All providers are invited to take part in a voluntary post-inspection survey in order to contribute to inspection development.

165. The great majority of our work is carried out smoothly and without incident. If concerns do arise during the inspection, they should be raised with the inspector as soon as possible, in order to resolve issues before the inspection is completed. Any concerns raised, and actions taken, will be recorded in the inspection evidence.

166. If it is not possible to resolve concerns during the inspection or through submitting comments in response to the draft report, the provider may wish to lodge a formal complaint on receipt of the final report. The inspector will ensure that the provider is informed that it is able to make a formal complaint and that information about how to complain is available on GOV.UK.

Part 2. The evaluation schedule – how early years settings will be judged

Background to the evaluation schedule

167. The evaluation schedule must be used in conjunction with the guidance set out in Part 1 of this document, 'How we will inspect early years providers', and in the EIF.

168. Paragraphs 12 to 15 set out our approach to reaching final judgements within the COVID-19 context.

169. The evaluation schedule is not exhaustive. It does not replace the professional judgement of inspectors. Inspectors must interpret grade descriptors in relation to children's age, development and stage of education.

170. In line with the EIF, inspectors will make the following judgements:

- overall effectiveness
- the quality of education
- behaviour and attitudes
- personal development
- leadership and management

171. The criteria for each of these judgements are drawn from Ofsted's inspection experience, areas of consensus in academic research, and research that Ofsted has itself undertaken (see 'Education inspection framework: overview of research').

172. Inspectors use a 4-point scale to make all judgements.

- grade 1: outstanding
- grade 2: good
- grade 3: requires improvement
- grade 4: inadequate

173. Inspectors must use their professional judgement to interpret and apply the grade descriptors to the setting they are inspecting. In doing so, they consider the following factors:

- a childminder who has only a very small number of children

- settings in which only babies and very young children are present
- settings that provide for funded 2-year-olds or groups who may be disadvantaged
- settings that have children who receive their main EYFS experience elsewhere
- children who are no longer in the early years age range

174. Inspectors must note any differences in the quality of education for children of different ages.[footnote 11] They will use their professional judgement and take into account all their evidence and give clear reasons for their judgements.

Reaching a judgement of outstanding

175. Outstanding is a challenging and exacting judgement. In order to reach this standard, inspectors will determine whether the early years provision meets all the criteria set out under 'good' for that judgement and does so securely and consistently. In other words, it is not enough that the provision is strong against some aspects of the judgement and not against others: it must meet each and every criterion. In addition, there are further criteria set out under the outstanding judgement, all of which the provision will also need to meet. Provision should only be judged 'outstanding' in a particular area if it is performing exceptionally, and this exceptional performance in that area is consistent and secure across the whole provision.

Reaching a judgement of good, requires improvement or inadequate

176. When considering a judgement of good or requires improvement inspectors will consider whether the overall quality of the provision is most closely aligned to the descriptions they set out. Inspectors are likely to reach a judgement of inadequate under a particular judgement if one or more of the inadequate criteria applies.

Overall effectiveness: the quality and standards of the early years provision

177. Inspectors must use all their evidence to evaluate what it is like to be a child in the provision. In making their judgements about a provider's overall effectiveness, inspectors will consider whether the standard of education and care is good. If it meets all the criteria for good, then inspectors will consider whether it is outstanding. If it is not good, then inspectors will consider whether it requires improvement or is inadequate.

178. In judging the overall effectiveness, inspectors will take account of the 4 judgements. They will also make a judgement about the effectiveness of the arrangements for safeguarding children.

179. Inspectors should take account of all the judgements made across the evaluation schedule. In particular, they should consider:

- the extent to which leaders and providers plan, design and implement the EYFS curriculum
- the extent to which the curriculum and care practices that the setting provides meet the needs of the range of children who attend, particularly children with SEND
- the progress children make in their learning and development relative to their starting points, and their readiness for the next stage of their education
- children's personal and emotional development, including whether they feel safe and are secure and happy
- whether the requirements for children's safeguarding and welfare have been fully met and there is a shared understanding of and responsibility for protecting children
- the effectiveness of leadership and management in evaluating practice and securing continuous development that improves children's education

Grade descriptors for the provision's overall effectiveness

Outstanding (1)

- The quality of education is outstanding.
- All other judgements are likely to be outstanding. In exceptional circumstances, one of the judgements may be good, as long as there is

convincing evidence that it is improving this area rapidly and securely towards outstanding.

- Safeguarding is effective.
- There are no breaches of EYFS requirements.

Good (2)

- The quality of education is at least good.
- All other judgements are likely to be good or outstanding. In exceptional circumstances, one of the judgement areas may require improvement, as long as there is convincing evidence that it is improving it rapidly and securely towards good.
- Safeguarding is effective.

Requires improvement (3)

- Where one or more aspects of the provision's work requires improvement, the overall effectiveness is likely to require improvement.
- Safeguarding is effective and any weaknesses are easy to rectify because they do not leave children at risk of harm.
- If there are any breaches of EYFS requirements, they do not have a significant impact on children's safety, well-being or learning and development.

Inadequate (4)

The provision's overall effectiveness is likely to be inadequate if one or more of the following apply.

- Safeguarding is ineffective.
- Any one of the judgements is inadequate.
- Breaches of EYFS requirements have a significant impact on the safety and well-being and/or the learning and development of the children.
- It has been given 2 previous 'requires improvement' judgements and it is still not good.

Quality of education

The EYFS curriculum

180. The EYFS (educational programmes) provides the curriculum framework that leaders build on to decide what they intend children to learn and develop.[footnote 12] Leaders and practitioners decide how to implement the curriculum so that children make progress in the 7 areas of learning. Leaders and

practitioners evaluate the impact of the curriculum by checking what children know and can do.

Curriculum flexibility

181. Some providers offer a specialist early years curriculum and Ofsted recognises their autonomy to do so. For example, they may follow a specific philosophical or pedological approach or reflect a particular faith. The choice of teaching methods is a decision for providers, within the confines of the EYFS. Alongside any specialist education provided, it is important that children have access to a highly ambitious, broad and rich curriculum.

182. When reaching a judgement on quality of education, inspectors will work with leaders and managers to understand how the curriculum as a whole is structured, and where they can find evidence that the quality of education criteria are met.

183. The inspector will judge fairly those providers that take radically different approaches to the curriculum and will judge the quality of the provision in relation to the impact it has on children's learning, development and well-being. Inspectors will assess any provider's curriculum favourably when leaders and managers have built a curriculum with appropriate coverage, content, structure and sequencing and have implemented it effectively. They are, however, likely to assess it negatively where the specialist curriculum has been designed or is being delivered in a way that limits children's opportunities or fails to prepare them for life in modern Britain.

184. Inspectors will evaluate how well:

- leaders assure themselves that the setting's curriculum (educational programmes) intentions are met and it is sufficiently challenging for the children it serves
- leaders use additional funding, including the early years pupil premium where applicable, and measure its impact on disadvantaged children's outcomes.
- practitioners ensure that the content, sequencing and progression in the areas of learning are secured and whether they demand enough of children
- children develop, consolidate and deepen their knowledge, understanding and skills across the areas of learning
- the provider's curriculum prepares children for their next stage

185. Teaching should not be taken to imply a 'top down' or formal way of working. It is a broad term that covers the many different ways in which adults help young children learn. It includes their interactions with children during planned and child-initiated play and activities, communicating and modelling language, showing,

explaining, demonstrating, exploring ideas, encouraging, questioning, recalling, providing a narrative for what they are doing, facilitating and setting challenges. It takes account of the equipment that adults provide and the attention given to the physical environment, as well as the structure and routines of the day that establish expectations. Integral to teaching is how practitioners assess what children know, understand and can do, as well as taking account of their interests and dispositions to learn (characteristics of effective learning), and how practitioners use this information to plan children's next steps in learning and to monitor their progress.

Cultural capital

186. Cultural capital is the essential knowledge that children need to prepare them for their future success.[footnote 13] It is about giving children the best possible start to their early education. As part of making a judgement about the quality of education, inspectors will consider how well leaders use the curriculum to enhance the experience and opportunities available to children, particularly the most disadvantaged.

187. Some children arrive at an early years settings with different experiences from others, in their learning and play. What a setting does, through its EYFS curriculum and interactions with practitioners, potentially makes all the difference for children. It is the role of the setting to help children experience the awe and wonder of the world in which they live, through the 7 areas of learning.

Grade descriptors for the quality of education

188. Inspectors will not grade intent, implementation and impact separately. Instead, inspectors will reach a single graded judgement for the quality of education, drawing on all the evidence they have gathered, using their professional judgement.

189. To reach a judgement about the quality of education, inspectors must use their professional judgement to consider the ages, development and stages of children in the setting.

190. In order for the quality of education to be judged outstanding, it must meet all of the good criteria securely and consistently. It must also meet all the outstanding criteria.

Outstanding (1)

The provider meets all the criteria for a good quality of education securely and consistently. The quality of education at this setting is exceptional. In addition, the following apply:

- The provider's curriculum intent and implementation are embedded securely and consistently across the provision. It is evident from what practitioners do that they have a firm and common understanding of the provider's curriculum intent and what it means for their practice. Across all parts of the provision, practitioners' interactions with children are of a high quality and contribute well to delivering the curriculum intent.
- Children's experiences over time are consistently and coherently arranged to build cumulatively sufficient knowledge and skills for their future learning.
- The impact of the curriculum on what children know, can remember and do is highly effective. Children demonstrate this through being deeply engaged in their work and play and sustaining high levels of concentration. Children, including those children from disadvantaged backgrounds, do well. Children with SEND achieve the best possible outcomes.
- Children consistently use new vocabulary that enables them to communicate effectively. They speak with increasing confidence and fluency, which means that they secure strong foundations for future learning, especially in preparation for them to become fluent readers.

191. Inspectors will use their professional judgement and adopt a 'best fit' approach in order to judge whether an early years provider is good or requires improvement.

Good (2)

Intent

- Leaders adopt or construct a curriculum that is ambitious and designed to give children, particularly the most disadvantaged, the knowledge and cultural capital they need to succeed in life.
- The provider's curriculum is coherently planned and sequenced. It builds on what children know and can do, towards cumulatively sufficient knowledge and skills for their future learning.
- The provider has the same ambitions for almost all children. For children with particular needs, such as those with high levels of SEND, their curriculum is still ambitious and meets their needs.

Implementation

- Children benefit from meaningful learning across the EYFS curriculum.

- Practitioners understand the areas of learning they teach and the way in which young children learn. Leaders provide effective support, including for staff with less experience and knowledge of teaching.
- Practitioners present information clearly to children, promoting appropriate discussion about the subject matter being taught. They communicate well to check children's understanding, identify misconceptions and provide clear explanations to improve their learning. In so doing, they respond and adapt their teaching as necessary.
- Practitioners ensure that their own speaking, listening and reading of English enables children to hear and develop their own language and vocabulary well. They read to children in a way that excites and engages them, introducing new ideas, concepts and vocabulary.
- Over the EYFS, teaching is designed to help children remember long-term what they have been taught and to integrate new knowledge into larger concepts.
- Practitioners and leaders use assessment well to check what children know and can do to inform teaching. This includes planning suitably challenging activities and responding to specific needs. Leaders understand the limitations of assessment and avoid unnecessary burdens for staff or children.
- Practitioners and leaders create an environment that supports the intent of an ambitious and coherently planned and sequenced curriculum. The available resources meet the children's needs and promote their focus on learning.
- Practitioners share information with parents about their child's progress in relation to the EYFS. They help parents to support and extend their child's learning at home, including how to encourage a love of reading.

Impact

- Children develop detailed knowledge and skills across the 7 areas of learning and use these in an age-appropriate way. Children develop their vocabulary and understanding of language across the EYFS curriculum.
- Children are ready for the next stage of education, especially school, where applicable. They have the knowledge and skills they need to benefit from what school has to offer when it is time to move on.
- Children enjoy, listen attentively and respond with comprehension to familiar stories, rhymes and songs that are appropriate to their age and stage of development.
- Children understand securely the early mathematical concepts appropriate to their age and stage that will enable them to move on to the next stage of learning.
- Children articulate what they know, understand and can do in an age-appropriate way, holding thoughtful conversations with adults and their friends.
- From birth onwards, children are physically active in their play, developing their physiological, cardiovascular and motor skills. They

show good control and coordination in both large and small movements appropriate for their stage of development.

Requires improvement (3)

- Provision is not good.
- Any breaches of the statutory requirements do not have a significant impact on children's learning and development.

Inadequate (4)

The quality of education is likely to be inadequate if one or more of the following applies.

- A poorly designed and implemented curriculum does not meet children's needs. The needs of babies and young children are not met.
- Practitioners have a poor understanding of the areas of learning they teach and the way in which young children learn.
- Assessment is overly burdensome. It is unhelpful in determining what children know, understand and can do.
- Children are not well prepared for school or the next stage of their learning, particularly those who are in receipt of additional funding. Strategies for engaging parents are weak and parents do not know what their child is learning or how they can help them improve.
- Breaches of the statutory requirements have a significant impact on children's learning and development.

Behaviour and attitudes

192. Inspectors will consider the ways in which children demonstrate their attitudes and behaviour through the characteristics of effective learning:

- playing and exploring
- active learning
- creating and thinking critically

193. Although attendance at the setting is not mandatory, inspectors will explore how well providers work with parents to promote children's attendance so that the children form good habits for future learning. In particular, inspectors will consider the attendance of children for whom the provider receives early years pupil premium.

194. Inspectors will consider the extent to which leaders and practitioners support children's behaviour and attitudes, including how the provision helps children to manage their own feelings and behaviour, and how to relate to others.

195. To reach a judgement about children's behaviour and attitudes, inspectors must use their professional judgement to consider the ages, development and stages of children in the setting.

Grade descriptors for behaviour and attitudes

196. In order for behaviour and attitudes to be judged outstanding, it must meet all of the good criteria securely and consistently. It must also meet all the outstanding criteria.

Outstanding (1)

The provider meets all the criteria for good behaviour and attitudes securely and consistently. Behaviour and attitudes in this provision are exceptional.

In addition, the following apply.

- Children have consistently high levels of respect for others. They increasingly show high levels of confidence in social situations. They confidently demonstrate their understanding of why behaviour rules are in place and recognise the impact that their behaviour has on others.
- Children are highly motivated and are very eager to join in, share and cooperate with each other. They have consistently positive attitudes to their play and learning.
- Children demonstrate high levels of self-control and consistently keep on trying hard, even if they encounter difficulties. When children struggle with this, leaders and practitioners take intelligent, swift and highly effective action to support them.

197. Inspectors will use their professional judgement and adopt a 'best fit' approach in order to judge whether a provider is good or requires improvement.

Good (2)

- The provider has high expectations for children's behaviour and conduct. These expectations are commonly understood and applied consistently and fairly. This is reflected in children's positive behaviour and conduct. They are beginning to manage their own feelings and behaviour and to understand how these have an impact on others. When children struggle with regulating their behaviour, leaders and practitioners take appropriate action to support them. Children are developing a sense of right and wrong.

- Children demonstrate their positive attitudes to learning through high levels of curiosity, concentration and enjoyment. They listen intently and respond positively to adults and each other. Children are developing their resilience to setbacks and take pride in their achievements.
- Children benefit fully from the early education opportunities available to them by participating and responding promptly to requests and instructions from practitioners.
- Relationships among children, parents and staff reflect a positive and respectful culture. Children feel safe and secure.

Requires improvement (3)

- Children's behaviour and attitudes are not good.
- Any breaches of the statutory requirements do not have a significant impact on children's behaviour and attitudes.

Inadequate (4)

Children's behaviour and attitudes are likely to be inadequate if one or both of the following apply.

- Children's behaviour and attitudes to learning are poor. Their frequent lack of engagement in activities and/or poor behaviour lead to a disorderly environment that hinders children's learning and/or puts them and others at risk.
- Children persistently demonstrate poor self-control and a lack of respect for others, leading to children not feeling safe and secure.

Personal development

198. Inspectors will evaluate the extent to which the provision is successfully promoting children's personal development. Inspectors must use their professional judgement to consider the effectiveness of the provision on children's all-round development. In doing so, inspectors must be mindful of the ages and stages of development of the children in the setting.

Grade descriptors for personal development

199. In order for personal development to be judged outstanding, it must meet all of the good criteria securely and consistently. It must also meet all the outstanding criteria.

Outstanding (1)

The provider meets all the criteria for good personal development securely and consistently. Personal development in this provision is exceptional. In addition, the following apply.

- The provider goes beyond the expected and is highly successful at giving children a rich set of experiences that promote an understanding of, and respect for, people, families and communities beyond their own. Opportunities for all children to develop their talents and interests are of exceptional quality.
- The provider ensures that these rich experiences are planned in a coherent way in the curriculum and they considerably strengthen the provider's offer.
- The way the provider goes about developing children's character is exemplary and is worthy of being shared with others.

*

200. Inspectors will use their professional judgement and adopt a 'best fit' approach in order to judge whether an early years provider is good or requires improvement.

Good (2)

- The curriculum and the provider's effective care practices promote and support children's emotional security and development of their character. Children are gaining a good understanding of what makes them unique.
- The curriculum and the provider's effective care practices promote children's confidence, resilience and independence. Practitioners teach children to take appropriate risks and challenges as they play and learn both inside and outdoors, particularly supporting them to develop physical and emotional health.
- A well-established key person system helps children form secure attachments and promotes their well-being and independence. Practitioners teach children the language of feelings, helping them to appropriately develop their emotional literacy (see pages 8 to 9 of the 'Statutory framework for the early years foundation stage (applies from 1 September 2021)', which set out the personal, social and emotional development (PSED) area of learning). Relationships between staff and babies are sensitive, stimulating and responsive.
- Practitioners provide a healthy diet and a range of opportunities for physically active play, both inside and outdoors. They give clear and consistent messages to children that support healthy choices around food, rest, exercise and screen time.
- Practitioners help children to gain an effective understanding of when they might be at risk, including when using the internet, digital technology and social media and where to get support if they need it.

- Practitioners ensure that policies are implemented consistently. Hygiene practices ensure that the personal needs of children of all ages are met appropriately. Practitioners teach children to become increasingly independent in managing their personal needs.
- Practitioners value and promote equality and diversity and prepare children for life in modern Britain. They do this in an age-appropriate way to help children to reflect on their differences and understand what makes them unique. Practitioners do this by: teaching children to be respectful and to recognise those who help us, and contribute positively to society; developing children's understanding of fundamental British values; developing children's understanding and appreciation of diversity; celebrating what we have in common; and routinely challenging stereotypical behaviours and promoting respect for different people.

Requires improvement (3)

- Provision to support children's personal development is not good.
- Any breaches of the statutory requirements for safeguarding and welfare and/or learning and development do not have a significant impact on children's safety, well-being and personal development.

Inadequate (4)

Personal development is likely to be inadequate if one or more of the following applies.

- Breaches of the statutory requirements have a significant impact on children's safety, well-being and personal development.
- Practitioners do not support children's social and emotional well-being or prepare them for transitions within the setting and/or to other settings and school.
- The key person system does not work effectively to support children's emotional well-being and children fail to form secure attachments with their carers. Babies are not stimulated.
- Policies, procedures and practice do not promote the health and welfare of children. As a result, children do not know how to keep themselves safe and healthy.
- Children have a narrow experience that does not promote their understanding of people and communities beyond their own or help them to recognise and accept each other's differences.

Leadership and management

201. Inspectors will evaluate evidence from the range of different inspection activities set out in Part 1 of the handbook when considering the effectiveness of leadership and management.

202. Inspectors must use their professional judgement to interpret and apply the grade descriptors for leadership and management for childminders.

Grade descriptors for leadership and management

203. In order for leadership and management to be judged outstanding, it must meet all of the good criteria securely and consistently. It must also meet all the outstanding criteria.

Outstanding (1)

The provider meets all the criteria for good leadership and management securely and consistently. Leadership and management in this provision is exceptional. In addition, the following apply.

- Leaders ensure that they and practitioners receive focused and highly effective professional development. Practitioners' subject, pedagogical content and knowledge consistently builds and develops over time, and this consistently translates into improvements in the teaching of the curriculum.
- Leaders ensure that highly effective and meaningful engagement takes place with staff at all levels and that any issues are identified. When issues are identified – in particular about workload – they are consistently dealt with appropriately and quickly.
- Staff consistently report high levels of support for well-being issues.

204. Inspectors will use their professional judgement and adopt a 'best fit' approach in order to judge whether an early years provider is good or requires improvement.

Good (2)

- Leaders have a clear and ambitious vision for providing high-quality, inclusive care and education to all. This is realised through strong shared values, policies and practice.
- Leaders focus on improving practitioners' knowledge of the areas of learning and understanding of how children learn to enhance the teaching of the curriculum and appropriate use of assessment. The practice and subject knowledge of practitioners (including those who are newly qualified) build and improve over time. Leaders have effective systems in place for the supervision and support of staff.
- Leaders act with integrity to ensure that all children, particularly those with SEND, have full access to their entitlement to early education.

- Leaders engage effectively with children, their parents and others in their community, including schools and other local services.
- Leaders engage with their staff and are aware of the main pressures on them. They are realistic and constructive in the way they manage staff. including their workload, to avoid any unnecessary burdens.
- Those with oversight or governance understand their role and carry this out effectively. They have a clear vision and strategy and hold senior leaders to account for the quality of care and education. They ensure that resources are managed sustainably, effectively and efficiently.
- The provider fulfils its statutory duties, for example under the Equality Act 2010, and other duties, for example in relation to the 'Prevent' strategy and safeguarding.
- Leaders protect staff from harassment, bullying and discrimination.
- The provider has a culture of safeguarding that facilitates effective arrangements to: identify children who may need early help or are at risk of neglect, abuse, grooming or exploitation; help children to reduce their risk of harm by securing the support they need, or referring in a timely way to those who have the expertise to help; and manage safe recruitment and allegations about adults who may be a risk to children.

Requires improvement (3)

- Leadership and management are not yet good.
- Any breaches of statutory requirements do not have a significant impact on children's safety, well-being or learning and development.

Inadequate (4)

Leadership and management are likely to be inadequate if one or more of the following applies.

- Leaders do not have the capacity to improve the quality of education and care. Actions taken to tackle areas of identified weakness have been insufficient or ineffective. Training for staff is ineffective.
- Leaders are not doing enough to tackle the poor curriculum or teaching, or the inappropriate use of assessment. This has a significant impact on children's progress, particularly those who are disadvantaged and those with SEND.
- Links with parents, other settings and professionals involved in supporting children's care and education do not identify or meet children's individual needs. Children fail to thrive.
- Leaders do not tackle instances of discrimination. Equality, diversity and British values are not actively promoted in practice.
- Safeguarding and welfare requirements are not met. Breaches have a significant impact on the safety and well-being of children.

Annex A. Inspecting before- and after-school care and holiday provision

1. Please refer to the section 'Inspection during the COVID-19 (coronavirus) pandemic', which outlines how our approach to inspection will reflect the COVID-19 context and the disruption caused to many education providers.

2. Providers (including childminders) registered on the Early Years Register but that only provide care exclusively for children at the beginning and end of the school day or in holiday periods will be inspected without receiving grades against the 4 judgements ('Quality of education', 'Behaviour and attitudes', 'Personal development' and 'Leadership and management') of the inspection framework.

3. These providers do not need to meet the learning and development requirements of the EYFS. They do have to meet in full the safeguarding and welfare requirements, which are designed to help providers create high-quality settings which are welcoming, safe and stimulating, and where children are able to grow in confidence.

4. The inspector will make a judgement only on the 'Overall effectiveness: quality and standards of the early years provision'. The inspection will result in one of 3 possible outcomes:

- met
- not met with actions
- not met with enforcement

5. The inspector will consider the criteria for 3 of the key judgements ('Behaviour and attitudes', 'Personal development' and 'Leadership and management') in reaching a judgement about whether or not the provider is meeting the safeguarding and welfare requirements of the EYFS.

6. When the provider does not meet one or more of the safeguarding and welfare requirements, the inspector must consider a judgement of 'not met' and either issue actions for the provider to take or consider enforcement action. In these cases, the inspector must follow the guidance for inadequate judgements set out previously in this handbook.

7. Provision judged as 'not met' will normally be re-inspected within 12 months.

8. When inspecting before and after school, and holiday care provision, the inspector must assess whether the provider:

- has premises suitable to care for children in the early years age range (as appropriate)
- can demonstrate sufficient understanding of the safeguarding and welfare requirements of the EYFS
- can meet the care, safeguarding and welfare needs of children

9. Providers must confirm that they meet the requirements of the Childcare Register, if applicable.

10. The provider must demonstrate how they:

- meet the safeguarding and welfare requirements
- safeguard children
- work in partnership with parents, carers and others
- offer an inclusive service
- evaluate their service and strive for continuous improvement

11. The provider should tell the inspector how they have addressed any actions from the last inspection and how this will improve the provision for children's care and learning.

Gathering and recording evidence

12. To assess whether the provider is meeting the safeguarding and welfare requirements, the inspector will undertake appropriate inspection activity as set out in part 1 of the handbook. In particular, inspectors will:

- observe interactions between practitioners and children
- consider how leaders and practitioners create and plan the play environment
- find out how practitioners seek children's views and engage them in planning of activities
- talk with practitioners about performance management and professional development
- met with the provider and/or their representative
- evaluate a sample of policies and procedures and relevant documentation
- where possible, seek the views of parents

Writing the report

13. Although there are no separate supporting judgements, the inspection will result in a summary for parents, which will explain what it is like for a child to attend the setting.

14. Inspectors will report on what the setting does well and what it needs to do better. This section must include reference to leadership and management, children's behaviour and attitudes and personal development. It must describe clearly any weaknesses that led to a 'not met' judgement and from which actions or enforcement action have been raised. Where a setting has a 'met' judgement, inspectors will usually report on what the setting needs to do better, but will not raise recommendations.

1. Ofsted defines the transitional period as the period for which transitional arrangements for schools remain in place. These are intended to be reviewed in March 2022.
2. The Secretary of State for Education decided that the EYFS profile assessment was not mandatory for any provider until 31 August 2021. However, all providers were required to use their 'best endeavours' to complete it and provide the information to Year 1 teachers and to parents, if this was possible. The EYFS profile was disapplied and a 'best endeavours' requirement introduced for the academic year 2020 to 2021 only.
3. Enforcement requires the provider to take action to remain compliant with the requirements of the 'Statutory framework for the early years foundation stage'. Our enforcement actions are set out in our 'Early years compliance handbook', April 2019.
4. In a situation where a childminder is self-isolating and as a result has no children present, they should make Ofsted aware during the notification call or a soon as self-isolation commences following notification.
5. Some providers do not have to deliver the learning and development requirements. See the Statutory framework for the early years foundation stage.
6. See 'Registering school-based provision'.
7. In a situation where a childminder is self-isolating and as a result has no children present, they should make Ofsted aware during the notification call or a soon as self-isolation starts following notification.
8. Chapter 5 of the 'Special educational needs and disability code of practice: 0–25 years' outlines the action that early years providers should take to meet their duties in relation to identifying and supporting all children with special educational needs (SEN), whether or not they have an education, health and care (EHC) plan.
9. This includes any staff or children currently self-isolating due to COVID-19.

10. See The Early Years Foundation Stage (Exemptions from Learning and Development Requirements) Regulations 2008; and The Early Years Foundation Stage (Exemptions from Learning and Development Requirements) (Amendment) Regulations 2012.

11. The term 'children' should be read to include the different ages and stages of children in the early years age range (birth to 31 August following a child's fifth birthday). Inspectors should interpret the grade descriptors according to a child's age and stage of development, therefore taking into account babies and young children.

12. The EYFS sets the standards that all early years providers must meet to ensure that children learn and develop well and are kept healthy and safe.

13. Cultural capital is the essential knowledge that children need to be educated citizens.

YOUR NOTES

YOUR NOTES

YOUR NOTES

YOUR NOTES

YOUR NOTES

Adapted and published by GRANGIS under the OGL Licence.
GRANGIS - UK PUBLISHING 2022.
Thank you for taking the time to leave us a review regarding this version

★★★★★

For further inquiries, please feel free to contact us at:
www.grangis.com / contact@grangis.com

www.ingramcontent.com/pod-product-compliance
Lightning Source LLC
LaVergne TN
LVHW060214210926
848481LV00008B/2736
* 9 7 9 8 8 8 5 5 9 0 8 7 7 *